RED, WHITE, BLUE AND BRAVE

A SALUTE TO AMERICA'S TROOPS

EDITED BY

Susan M. Moyer

SP L.L.C.

PUBLISHER
PETER L. BANNON

EDITOR
SUSAN M. MOYER

BOOK DESIGN
JENNIFER L. POLSON

COVER DESIGN
K. JEFFREY HIGGERSON

PHOTO IMAGING
TRACY GAUDREAU,
CHRISTINE F. MOHRBACHER,
AND KENNETH J. O'BRIEN

COPY EDITOR
CYNTHIA L. MCNEW

All photographs are from AP/Wide World Photos.

ISBN 1-58261-729-5

INTRODUCTION

"All that is necessary for evil to triumph is for good men to do nothing."

Edmund Burke

In the aftermath of September 11, 2001, the United States pioneered the construction of a coalition that currently includes some 90 nations pursuing a global war against terrorism. Around the world, countries have contributed in a variety of ways—some militarily, others diplomatically, economically and financially. Some nations have helped openly; others have chosen not to disclose their contributions. This coalition's stated purpose is to defeat terrorism, wherever it may exist.

At the conclusion of Operation Desert Storm in 1991, Saddam Hussein continued to rule Iraq. Over a decade later, President George W. Bush led a push for thorough U.N. inspections to determine if Iraq possessed weapons of mass destruction, a violation of U.N. resolutions. Amid much international debate, President Bush gave Saddam Hussein a 48-hour deadline on March 17 to leave Iraq or face war waged by the United States and a number of other coalition countries.

The war in Iraq became a daily reality for Americans, with constant updates on the internet and on live television. We were presented with real-time war for the first time in history. Anti-war protests competed with troop support rallies for attention on Main Streets across the country.

Whether we supported or opposed the decision to go to war in Iraq, or our president, or U.S. foreign policies, Americans agreed on one thing: those were our neighbors, brothers, sisters, husbands and wives in harm's way, and we loved and appreciated them.

Red, White, Blue and Brave: A Salute to America's Troops honors the everyday heroes who traveled to the other side of the world to uphold the principles that America stands for: liberty, justice and freedom. We believe that all people are entitled to enjoy peace and prosperity under those same guiding values. Throughout history, we've turned to the American soldier to protect our nation and preserve these principles we hold dear. For that, men and women of the armed forces, we salute you.

SUSAN M. MOYER, EDITOR

TIMELINE:
OPERATION IRAQI FREEDOM

August 2, 1990
Iraq invades Kuwait. The UN Security Council calls for a full withdrawal.

August 6, 1990
The UN imposes economic sanctions on Iraq.

January 17, 1991
The Gulf War starts as coalition forces begin bombing Iraq.

February 24, 1991
Ground invasion of Iraq and Kuwait begins. Kuwait is liberated three days later.

June 27, 1993
U.S. forces fire cruise missiles at an Iraqi intelligence building in Baghdad, in response to the attempted assassination of former President George Bush in Kuwait in April.

March-June, 1996
UN inspection teams are denied access to sensitive areas.

June, 1996
A CIA-backed coup attempt against Saddam Hussein is foiled. Participants are executed by Saddam.

October 29, 1997
Iraq demands that Americans on the UN inspection team leave; they go but return on November 20.

January 13-22, 1998
Iraq withdraws cooperation with UN inspectors, claiming some are British and American spies.

November 14, 1999
Iraq allows inspections to resume.

December 16, 1999
UN inspection teams are withdrawn, after concluding that Iraq is not cooperating fully.

December 16-19, 1999
U.S. and Britain launch bombing campaign Operation Desert Fox to destroy suspected weapons of mass destruction.

November, 2000
Iraq rejects new weapons inspections proposals.

February, 2001
Britain and U.S. planes launch raids to try to disable Iraq's air defense network.

January 30, 2002
President Bush says Iraq is part of an "axis of evil" during his State of the Union address.

September 12, 2002
President Bush, addressing the UN General Assembly, challenges the UN to confront the "grave and gathering danger" of Iraq or stand aside as the United States and other nations act.

September 16, 2002
Iraq says it will allow international weapons inspectors to return "without conditions."

September 30, 2002
UN and Iraq discuss terms for weapons inspections. Talks leave eight presidential compounds off limits, and U.S. seeks authorization for a use of force if Iraq fails to comply with inspections.

October 10, 2002
Congress adopts joint resolution authorizing use of force against Iraq.

November 8, 2002
UN Security Council unanimously adopts Resolution 1441, which outlines an enhanced inspection regime for Iraq's disarmament to be conducted by the IAEA.

January 16, 2003
Weapons inspections chiefs report to the Security Council that while Iraq has provided access to facilities, concerns remain regarding undeclared material, inability to interview Iraqi scientists, inability to conduct aerial surveillance during inspections, and harassment of inspectors.

January 28, 2003
Bush says Saddam Hussein "is not disarming. To the contrary, he is deceiving," during his State of the Union address to Congress. "He has shown utter contempt for the United Nations and the opinion of the world," Bush says.

March 17, 2003
The U.S. and Britain withdraw their drafted Security Council resolution and advise weapons inspectors to evacuate Iraq. During a televised address, President Bush issues an ultimatum to Saddam Hussein to leave Iraq within 48 hours or face war. Saddam refuses.

March 19, 2003
Operation Iraqi Freedom begins.

RESPONSIBILITY

"We're in a **fight** for our principles, and our first responsibility is to **live** by them."

GEORGE W. BUSH

AWARENESS

"To see the right

and not to do it is

cowardice."

CONFUCIUS (551-478 B.C.)

During Operation Iraqi Freedom, the Air Force flew more than 30,000 sorties, including 12,000 strike sorties, and dropped more than 21,300 munitions, 70 percent of which were precision-guided. Tankers flew more than 17,050 refueling missions supporting aircraft from all services. ISR assets, including JSTARS, UAVs, Rivet Joint, U-2, AWACS and Commando Solo, flew more than 3,025 missions, providing persistent battlefield awareness.

FREEDOM

"Freedom isn't free."

QUOTED BY
GENERAL TOMMY FRANKS

LEFT

General Tommy R. Franks is the Commander in Chief, United States Central Command, MacDill Air Force Base, Florida. General Franks's awards include the Defense Distinguished Service Medal; Distinguished Service Medal (two awards); Legion of Merit (four awards); Bronze Star Medal with "V" (three awards); Purple Heart (three awards); Air Medal with "V"; Army Commendation Medal with "V"; and a number of U.S. and foreign service awards. He wears the Army General Staff Identification Badge and the Aircraft Crewmember's Badge.

"The history of every country begins in the heart of a man or woman."

Willa Cather

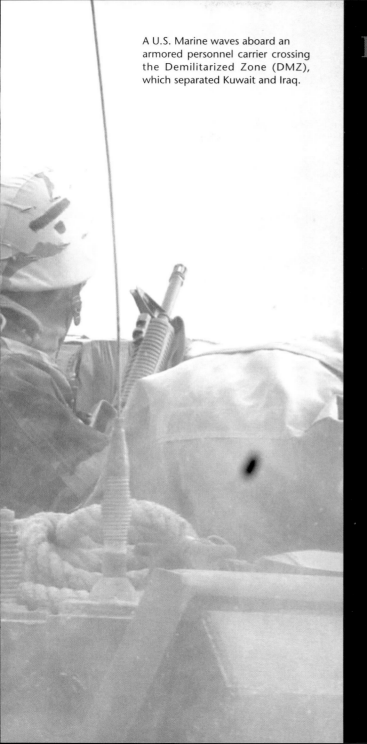

A U.S. Marine waves aboard an armored personnel carrier crossing the Demilitarized Zone (DMZ), which separated Kuwait and Iraq.

DISARMAMENT

"**The President** of the United States—our Commander in Chief—in agreement with the leadership of our coalition partners has ordered the initiation of combat operations. Our objectives are clear. We will disarm Iraq and remove the regime that has refused to disarm peacefully. . . . We will bring food, medicines, and other humanitarian assistance to Iraqis in need.

You have my highest personal **confidence** and the confidence of your Commander in Chief. You are now in harm's way. Our task will not be easy, but we are fighting for a just cause and the outcome is not in doubt. I am proud of you—all that you have done and all you will achieve in the days ahead.

We will all do our duty. **May God bless** each of you, this coalition, and the United States of America."

GENERAL TOMMY FRANKS'S MESSAGE TO THE TROOPS ON MARCH 21, 2003, THE DAY THIS PHOTO WAS TAKEN

> "It takes the bravest of the brave to provide freedom to someone you don't know who lives half a world away. Keep your head down and come home soon!"

LETTER OF SUPPORT TO U.S. TROOPS

After consulting with Homeland Security Secretary Tom Ridge, the FBI, and the Secret Service, NCAA president Myles Brand announced that the NCAA basketball tournaments would proceed as scheduled. March Madness was set to begin with the first round of the men's tournament only one day after President Bush's deadline for Saddam Hussein to leave Iraq or face war. War updates preempted some early-round games, which were moved at the last minute to ESPN. Players and coaches showed their support for the troops by wearing yellow ribbons, pins, and American flag patches.

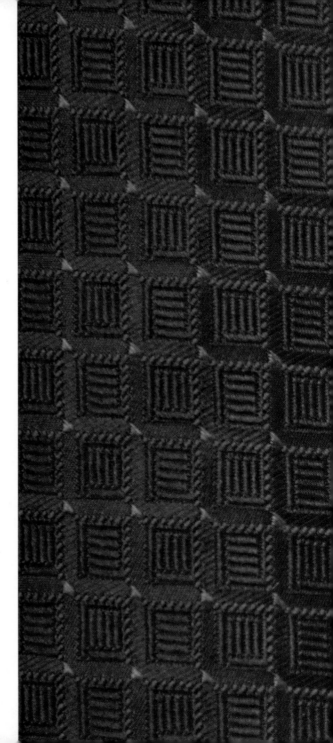

A manager on Florida's men's basketball team wears a yellow ribbon in support of the U.S. troops in Iraq during a second-round NCAA South Regional game against Michigan State in Tampa, Florida.

Dear Marine,

Hi, my name is Omar and I'm a seventh grader in Arcadia, California. I just wanted to say thanks for fighting for us. I'm really sorry for the Marines who passed away in this war. Good luck and come back peacefully. Bye.

P.S. Kick Butt.

Omar
Arcadia, California

LEFT

Adan Castillejos of San Diego, California, watches as F/A-18 Hornets are launched from the deck of the USS *Nimitz*.

"**Americans** are a free people, who know that freedom is the right of every person and the future of every nation. The liberty we prize is not America's gift to the world; it is **God's gift to humanity**."

"I shall know but one country. The ends I aim at shall be my country's, my God's and Truth's. I was born an American; **I live an American; I shall die an American.**"

Daniel Webster

TRADITION

"There is a tradition in the Corps that

no one who falls will be left behind

on the battlefield. Our country has a tradition, as well.

No one who falls will be forgotten by this grateful nation. We

honor their service to America and we pray their families will receive

God's comfort and God's grace."

GEORGE W. BUSH

RIGHT

The 4th Infantry Division soldiers walk toward a group of tanks
as dust envelops Camp Pennsylvania, about 25 miles from the
Iraqi border in Kuwait.

The 4th Infantry Division is the Army's First Digitized Division. It is the most lethal, modern, and deployable heavy division in the world prepared to conduct full-spectrum combat operations. The 4th Infantry Division nickname, the "Ivy Division," comes from the roman numeral four (IV). Their shoulder patch features four green ivy leaves joined at the stem and opening at the four corners. Ivy leaves are symbolic of tenacity and fidelity, and are the basis of the Division's motto, "Steadfast and Loyal."

A convoy of incoming U.S. military vehicles moves through the desert toward the border of Iraq after arriving in Kuwait.

"I have a message for the men and women who will keep the peace, members of the American Armed Forces:

Many of you are assembling in or near the Middle East, and some crucial hours may lie ahead. In those hours, the success of our cause will depend on you. Your training has prepared you. Your honor will guide you. You believe in America, and America believes in you.

GEORGE W. BUSH

ASSURANCE

"Let every nation know, whether it wishes us well or ill, that we shall pay any price, bear any burden, meet any hardship, support any friend, oppose any foe, to assure the **survival and success** of liberty."

John F. Kennedy

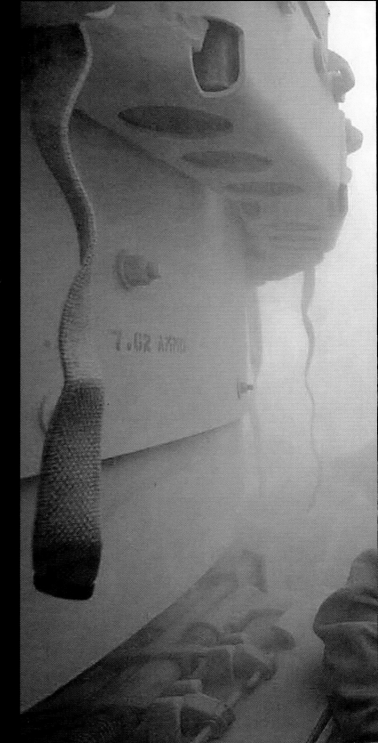

Early in the war in Iraq,

coalition aircraft dropped leaflets that explained to Iraqi military troops how to avoid being harmed by coalition troops in the case of an invasion.

The front of the leaflets read, "To avoid destruction, follow coalition guidelines," and showed a picture indicating that Iraqi troops should stay at least one kilometer from their vehicles. The back of the leaflet listed eight actions necessary to indicate surrender:

- Park vehicles in squares, no larger than battalion size.
- Stow artillery and Air Defense Systems in travel configuration.
- Display white flags on vehicles.
- No visible man-portable air defense systems.
- Personnel must gather in groups, a minimum of one kilometer away from their vehicles.
- Officers may retain their sidearms; others must disarm.
- Do not approach coalition forces.
- Wait for further instructions.

U.S. Army Specialist Neil Holihan, 23, from Fairfax, Virginia, with the A 3-7 Infantry Regiment, squints from the dust while looking out from a Bradley fighting vehicle, just after crossing the border into southern Iraq.

"Early in my life, my dad taught me the meaning of the flag and why we honor it. It has nothing to do with being Republican or Democrat. It has nothing to do with political meandering. It has EVERYTHING to do with the sacrifice that normal men and women give, in order that we may be free."

LETTER OF SUPPORT TO U.S. TROOPS

"Thank you for protecting our freedom, our country and the world. I realize the sacrifices you have made to protect us. Words cannot express the gratitude and pride I feel for people such as you. I am praying for your safe and quick return home. God bless you and God bless America!"

MESSAGE TO U.S. TROOPS IN IRAQ

OBJECTIVES

"Secretary of Defense Don Rumsfeld, my boss, outlined the military objectives of Operation Iraqi Freedom. Let me review them with you:

☆ **First,** end the regime of Saddam Hussein.

☆ **Second,** to identify, isolate and eliminate Iraq's weapons of mass destruction.

☆ **Third,** to search for, to capture and to drive out terrorists from that country.

☆ **Fourth,** to collect such intelligence as we can related to terrorist networks.

☆ **Fifth,** to collect such intelligence as we can related to the global network of illicit weapons of mass destruction.

☆ **Sixth,** to end sanctions and to immediately deliver humanitarian support to the displaced and to many needy Iraqi citizens.

☆ **Seventh,** to secure Iraq's oil fields and resources, which belong to the Iraqi people.

☆ **And last,** to help the Iraqi people create conditions for a transition to a representative self-government."

GENERAL TOMMY FRANKS, CENTRAL COMMAND BRIEFING

General Tommy Franks, commander of U.S. Central Command, visits the troops of the 1st Marines Expeditionary Force in Iraq.

COURAGE

"**Courage** is not the absence of fear, but rather the judgement that something else is more **important** than fear."

Ambrose Redmoon

LEFT

General Tommy Franks was named *Time* magazine's Person of the Week in early March 2002 for his role in leading U.S. troops in Afghanistan. *Time* said that Franks " . . . is insistently realistic, never gloating, understated about victory and reassuringly honest about its inevitable costs. Throw in a touch of folksiness, some of the aw-shucks collar-tugging of an old artillery man blinking in the spotlight's white glare, and you have a fine war hero indeed. A real general, with real American soldiers on the ground under his command, who realizes how fragile and precious a cargo that is."

35

U.S. Marines Private First Class Matthew D. Blair, assistant automatic rifleman with Fox Company, 2nd Battalion, 6th Marine Regiment, patrols the streets of a compound near central Iraq. Blair, 18, from Dayton, Ohio is among the Fox Company squad calling themselves the "Outlaws."

JUSTICE

"These are

high calling

of our nation a

world. Overco

noblest cause ar

And the libera

is the fulfillment

promise. The obje

war are worthy o

all the acts of

erosity that hav

again, we are app

country to ensur

serve the cause

will prevai

IDEALS

"**America** was established not to create wealth but to realize a vision, to realize an ideal —to discover and maintain **liberty** among men."

Woodrow Wilson

RIGHT

Trecia Tyson of Round Mountain clutches a photograph of her son, Army Sergeant James Tyson Jr., while saying the Pledge of Allegiance in Redding, California. Tyson is a combat engineer who is stationed in Iraq.

WHAT IS THE COALITION?

"Citizens from more than 80 countries died on 9/11/02—innocent men, women and children from across the globe. Within hours of the tragedy, coalitions involving many nations assembled to fight terrorism—literally hundreds of countries have contributed in a variety of ways—some militarily, others diplomatically, economically and financially. Some nations have helped openly; others prefer not to disclose their contributions.

The United States began building the coalition on September 12, 2001, and there are **over 90 nations supporting the global war on terrorism.** To date, 21 nations have deployed more than 16,000 troops to the U.S. Central Command's region of responsibility. This coalition of the willing is working hard every day to defeat terrorism, wherever it may exist.

The war against terrorism is a broad-based effort that will take time. Every nation has different circumstances and will participate in different ways. This mission and future missions will require a series of coalitions ready to take on the challenges and assume the risks associated with such an operation.

Coalition forces have made important contributions in the war against terrorism across the spectrum of operations. Particular contributions include, but are not limited to, providing vital intelligence, personnel, equipment and assets for use on the ground, air and sea.

Coalition members also have provided liaison teams, participated in planning, provided bases and granted over-flight permissions, as well as sizeable contributions of humanitarian assistance."

UNITED STATES CENTRAL COMMAND

SUCCESS

"PATRIOT-firing batteries successfully intercepted and destroyed two tactical ballistic missiles during an attack on Kuwait at approximately 12:24 p.m. and 1:30 p.m. The PATRIOT's guidance and control system locked onto the ballistic missiles, successfully engaging the targets with Hit to Kill PAC III and Guidance Enhanced Missiles (GEM). The PATRIOT missile system has been upgraded numerous times, affecting accuracy, lethality and the defended footprint. The PATRIOT system deployed on the battlefield today is the latest version, referred to as a PAC-3."

CENTRAL COMMAND BRIEFING ON THE IRAQI AIR ATTACKS
TAKING PLACE IN PHOTO ON MARCH 20, 2003

RIGHT

United States Army and Marine troops in a bunker at their base in the Kuwaiti desert during an air raid alert as missiles were launched by Iraq into Kuwait.

March 20, 2003

"In the long history of the world, only a few generations have been granted the role of defending freedom in its hour of maximum danger. I do not shrink from this responsibility—I welcome it."

John F. Kennedy

PATRIOTISM

"**Patriotism** is easy to understand in America; it means looking out for yourself by **looking out** for your country."

Calvin Coolidge

RIGHT

Thousands of union workers bearing American flags rally in support of U.S. military efforts in Iraq.

"One country, one constitution, one destiny."

Daniel Webster

First Lieutenant Eric Hooper from Albany, Georgia, with the U.S. Army A 3-7 Infantry looks through the dust after crossing into Iraq from Kuwait.

"The American people and the watching world are seeing another great generation. The citizens of Iraq, like so many oppressed peoples before them, are coming to know the kind of men and women that America sends forth to meet danger and to defend freedom."

VICE PRESIDENT DICK CHENEY

"A man's feet must be planted in his country,
but his eyes should survey the world."

George Santayana

RISK

"War is a very, very risky business for everybody. We are not over-confident about this endeavor. We are confident about the ultimate outcome of this endeavor. We are soldiers, sailors, air-men and marines in a combined, in a joint team that is very **powerful**, and one of the most integrated and well-trained forces ever put together. There won't be anything that stops us on the battlefield."

**LIEUTENANT GENERAL JOHN ABIZAID
DEPUTY COMMANDER,
COMBINED FORCES COMMAND**

LEFT

A convoy of the 3rd Brigade of the U.S. 101st Airborne Division prepares to move in the Kuwaiti desert.

"A man's country is not a certain area of land, of mountains, rivers, and woods, but it is a principle, and patriotism is loyalty to that principle."

GEORGE WILLIAM CURTIS

"One flag, one land, one heart, one hand, One Nation, evermore!"

Oliver Wendell Holmes

OURAGE

"**Courage** is the price that life
exacts for **granting peace.**"

Amelia Earhart

The 15th Marine Expeditionary Unit (Special Operations Capable), which was the first Marine force on the ground in Afghanistan at the start of Operation Enduring Freedom, began moving ashore at a port in Kuwait just after dawn February 12, 2003. The unit brought with it 2,000-plus highly trained Marines certified capable of completing numerous operations to include airfield seizures, tactical recoveries of personnel and aircraft, amphibious raids and humanitarian assistance.

A U.S. Marine with the 15th Marine Expeditionary Unit wearing a mask drinks water in the Kuwaiti desert near the border with Iraq.

"Our flag is our national design, pure and simple, behold it! Listen to it! Every star has a tongue, every stripe is articulate."

Robert Winthrop

An American soldier with the 173rd Airborne out of Vicenza, Italy, mans a heavy-caliber machine gun as a convoy of U.S. troops leaves from an airstrip near Harir, in Kurdish-held northern Iraq.

FEARLESSNESS

"**The fearless** are merely fearless.

People who act in spite of their fear are

truly brave."

James A. La Fond-Lewis

Central Command briefing excerpt from March 28, 2003:

"In the past 24 hours, we continued combat operations against regime forces, conducted strikes against regime command and control, and took major steps forward in setting the foundation for the future of Iraq. In places where we encounter paramilitary forces and terrorist-like death squads, we are inflicting severe blows. With each engagement, the regime loses more of its ability to deny freedom to the Iraqi people.

We remain very proud of our men and women for their determination and their resolve. The coalition continues to build capacity for future operations, while conducting a variety of operations in the present. As more nations commit themselves to this operation, their contributions and their efforts are incorporated, and the coalition gets stronger. We appreciate the role played by each."

BRIGADIER GENERAL VINCE BROOKS

Soldiers from the 3rd Brigade of the 101st Airborne assemble before leaving to move to forward positions at Camp New Jersey in the Kuwaiti desert.

BELIEF

"What constitutes an American? Not color nor race nor religion. Not the pedigree of his family nor the place of his birth. Not the coincidence of his citizenship. An American is one who loves justice and believes in the dignity of man. An American is one who will fight for his freedom and that of his neighbor. An American is one who will sacrifice property, ease, and security in order that he and his children may retain the rights of all free men. "

HAROLD ICKES

"I AM AN AMERICAN" SPEECH

PRIDE

"Sure I wave the **American flag**. Do you know a better flag to wave?

Sure I love **my country** with all her faults.

I'm not ashamed of that, never have been, never will be."

John Wayne

LEFT

Thousands of union workers bearing American flags rally in support of U.S. military efforts in Iraq.

NECESSITY

"**War** is just when it is necessary; arms are permissible when there is **no hope** except in arms."

Machiavelli, The Prince

RIGHT

The 3rd Brigade, 101st Airborne Division (Air Assault) traces its lineage back to the organization of Headquarters, 160th Infantry Brigade. While serving as part of the American Occupation Force, the Japanese gave the paratroopers of the 187th Infantry Regiment the nickname "Rakkasan," which loosely translated means "falling umbrella." The 3rd Brigade, 101st Airborne Division's motto is "ready to move and ready to fight."

Soldiers from the 3rd Brigade of the U.S. 101st Airborne Division rest in foxholes by their convoy in a staging area in the Kuwaiti desert.

OLD GLORY

"You, our best, brightest, and bravest, are in our thoughts today and every day.

From the Atlantic to the Pacific, Old Glory is still flying from cars and trucks, and is proudly displayed on count-less front porches and lapels in support of your dedication and devotion to duty."

LETTER OF SUPPORT TO U.S. TROOPS

LEFT

Steve Busico, five, son of U.S. Army Specialist Stefano Busico of the 101st Airborne Division, kneels down and looks at his small American flag as his family holds a larger flag adorned with family photographs during a rally in support of the troops in Iraq on Fort Campbell Blvd. in Clarksville, Tennessee.

"War is an ugly thing, but not the ugliest of things. The decayed and degraded state of moral and patriotic feeling which thinks that nothing is worth war is much worse. The person who has nothing for which he is willing to fight, nothing which is more important than his own personal safety, is a miserable creature, and has no chance of being free unless made or kept so by the exertions of better men than himself."

John Stuart Mill

U.S. Captain Bud Ford of Clarksville, Tennessee, center, briefs soldiers from the 3rd Brigade of the 101st Airborne Division in a staging area in the Kuwaiti desert.

PLEDGE

"The people of Iraq have lived in this nightmare world for more than two decades. It is understandable that fear and distrust run deep. I give this pledge to the citizens of Iraq: We're coming with a mighty force to end the reign of your oppressors. We are coming to bring you food and medicine and a better life. And we are coming, and we will not stop, we will not relent until your country is free."

GEORGE W. BUSH

U.S. soldiers wear their gas masks as they head to the Iraqi border in a convoy through the desert in northern Kuwait.

JUSTICE

"Throughout history it has been the inaction of those who could have acted, the indifference of those who should have known better, the silence of the voice of justice when it mattered most, that has made it possible for evil to triumph."

Haile Selassie

U.S. soldier Marrero Ricardo, 31, from Puerto Rico gives a flower to Iraqi Dilan Farman, two, in the town of Kirkuk, Iraq.

FREEDOM

"**Posterity**—you will never know

how much it has cost my generation to

preserve your freedom. I hope you will

make good use of it."

John Quincy Adams

RIGHT

Americans hold signs and U.S. flags during a rally
at the Veterans Memorial in Anchorage, Alaska
to show their support for the U.S. troops fighting in Iraq.

LIBERTY

"The name of American, which belongs to you in your national capacity, must always exalt the just **pride of patriotism** more than any appellation derived from local discriminations. With slight shades of difference, you have the same religion, manners, habits and political principles. You have in **common cause** fought and triumphed together. The **independence and liberty** you possess are the work of joint councils and joint efforts, of common dangers, sufferings, and **successes.**"

George Washington

LEFT

Ground Zero workers applaud as they watch thousands of nearby union workers bearing American flags rally in support of U.S. military efforts in Iraq.

DUTY

"When freedom needs defending, America turns to our military. And as they do their job, our men and women in uniform count on their families. This is a time of hardship for many military families. Some of you have been separated from your loved ones for quite a while because of long deployments. **All of America is grateful for your sacrifice.** Hundreds of reserve units across America have been activated in this time of war, and our country thanks these fine citizens and their employers for putting duty first."

GEORGE W. BUSH

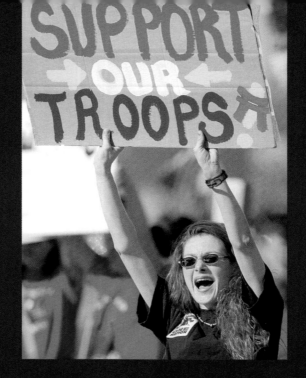

SUPPORT

"**My fellow citizens,** the dangers to our country and the world will be overcome. We will pass through this time of peril and carry on the work of peace. We will defend our freedom. We will bring freedom to others and we will prevail. May God bless our country and **all who defend her.**"

GEORGE W. BUSH

A deck of 55 playing cards that picture members of Iraqi leadership, including Saddam Hussein, were distributed among members of coalition forces to aid in finding and capturing former Iraqi leaders considered dangerous or guilty of military crimes. The Defense Intelligence Agency originally produced 200 decks to help U.S. troops identify Iraqi government officials. The playing cards captured the imagination of the American public, and hundreds of thousands of these decks have been sold in the United States.

LEFT

U.S. Brigadier General Vincent Brooks displays the deck of playing cards featuring members of the Iraqi leadership during a news conference at the Coalition Media Center, at Camp As Sayliyah, in Doha, Qatar.

"**America lives** in the heart of every man everywhere who wishes to find a region where **he will be free** to work out his destiny as he chooses."

Woodrow Wilson

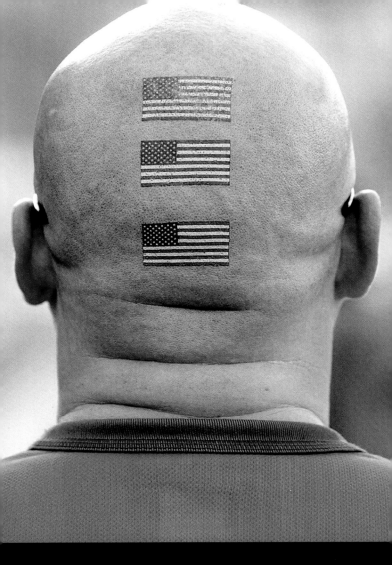

ast Saturday I attended a freedom rally to show support of our troops. There we
nd women there, young and old, even some kids. Don't believe for a second that
s and gals. I never attended a rally in my life, but I intend to attend every one in o
is resolved. We love you and appreciate you more than you know. God Bless yo

BLESSED

"Those who expect to reap the blessings of freedom must undergo the fatigue of supporting it."

Thomas Paine

EFFORT

"The meaning of America is not to be found in a life without toil. Freedom is not only bought with a great price; it is maintained by unremitting effort."

Calvin Coolidge

LEFT

The CH-53E Sea Stallion helicopter is the Marine Corps' heavy-lift vehicle, designed for the transportation of material and supplies, and is compatible with most amphibious-class ships. It can move more equipment over rugged terrain in bad weather and at night than its predecessors. It has consistently proven its worth to fleet commanders with its versatility and range. With four and one-half hours' endurance, this helicopter is capable of lifting 16 tons at sea level, transporting the load 50 nautical miles (57.5 miles) and returning. The Sea Stallion seats 37 passengers, and the unit replacement cost is $26.1 million.

A U.S. Marine tank rolls through the Republican Presidential Palace compound in Baghdad.

CHALLENGE

"The ultimate measure of a man is not where he stands in moments of comfort, but where he stands at times of challenge and controversy."

Martin Luther King, Jr.

The main building in the Republican Palace in Baghdad was built to be one of the most opulent buildings in the world. It was rebuilt by Saddam in defiance after the 1991 Gulf War, while much of Iraq was plunged into poverty.

A marble plaque inside reads: "Armies from thirty nations invaded and he [Saddam] emerged larger than life." Another plaque describes how engineers painstakingly restored the palace just one year after it was bombed in 1991.

Like the rest of Saddam's palaces—reportedly numbering in the dozens—everything in the Republican Presidential Palace is massive and ostentatious. Inside are gold doors and engraved wooden ceilings, and some bathrooms have gold fittings. Verses from the Koran and the emblem of a hawk decorate the outer walls.

In the Council of the People building, sayings authored by Saddam are engraved on the walls. Ironically, one reads: "If you get to govern then rule justly and do not let your whims influence your decisions."

RELIEF

"The coalition is committed to disarming Iraq. But the coalition is equally committed to bringing humanitarian assistance to the Iraqi people. Our humanitarian work in Iraq is only beginning. The U.S. military, coalition partners and other civilian organizations from around the world have positioned millions of meals, medicines and other supplies for the Iraqi people"

BRIGADIER GENERAL VINCE BROOKS

RIGHT

A U.S. Marine greets an Iraqi man as others surround him prior to the distribution of a shipment of humanitarian aid, in Safwan, Iraq.

GILANCE

"We are not weak, if we make proper use of those means which the God of nature hath placed in our power. The battle, sir, is not to the strong alone; it is to the vigilant, the active, the brave."

Patrick Henry

RIGHT

Under a full moon at dawn, a soldier from the U.S. Army's A Company 3rd Battalion 7th Infantry Regiment walks past a line of Bradley fighting vehicles.

LIBERATION

"To all the men and women of the United States Armed Forces

now in the Middle East, the peace of a troubled world and

the hopes of an oppressed people now depend on you. That trust is

well placed. The enemies you confront will come to know your

skill and bravery. The people you liberate will witness the honor-

able and decent spirit of the American military."

GEORGE W. BUSH

RIGHT

Captain Mike Johns, right, of Hampton, Virginia, shakes hands with Sheik Naseem Sheshoon in Atshan, southern Iraq, after discussing how American troops can help the impoverished farming community and how villagers can help U.S. forces root out remnants of the Saddam Hussein regime.

CHARACTER

"**Adversity** has revealed the character of our country, to the world and to ourselves. America is a strong nation, and **honorable** in the use of our strength. We exercise power without conquest, and we sacrifice for the **liberty of strangers.**"

GEORGE W. BUSH

RIGHT

Serving the military is nothing new for the pigeon. During World War II, pigeons were drafted into the Army Signal Corps to carry battlefield messages of grave urgency. In Iraq they served as an early warning system, according to U.S. chemical warfare specialists. The pigeons are carried in cages atop U.S. military Humvees to detect possible Iraqi chemical attacks. If the birds, riding with a caretaker, get sick, it might signal a chemical attack, giving Marines some time to don gas masks.

"**Throughout its history,** America has given hope, comfort and inspiration to freedom's cause in all lands. The **reservoir of goodwill** and respect for America was not built up by American arms or intrigue; it was built upon our deep dedication to the cause of **human liberty and welfare.**"

Adlai Stevenson

"Thanks does not seem to be enough. You have the support of millions of Americans. Although we have never met and probably will never meet, I feel as if I know every one of you, and I want to express my appreciation for all that you do. Godspeed, be safe."

LETTER OF SUPPORT TO U.S. TROOPS

Dear Marine Member,

Hello, my name is Breanne. I am 13 years old. I am writing to you today to tell you that my family and I support the troops. We are praying for your success and safe return. I think that all servicemen and women are very brave to risk their lives for our country.

God Bless You!

Sincerely,

Breanne

"We are a nation of many nationalities, many races, many religions—
bound together by a single unity, the unity of freedom and equality."

Franklin D. Roosevelt

"We are the standard-bearers in the only really authentic revolution, the democratic revolution against tyrannies. Our strength is not to be measured by our military capacity alone, by our industry, or by our technology. We will be remembered, not for the power of our weapons, but for the power of our compassion, our dedication to human welfare."

Hubert Humphrey

RIGHT

U.S. Army Private Adam Consider from Middletown, Rhode Island, with A Company 3rd Battalion 7th Infantry Regiment, searches through the brush in Baghdad.

MAKING A
DIFFERENCE

"Some people live an entire lifetime and wonder if they have ever made a difference in the world, but the Marines don't have that problem."

Ronald Reagan

Lance Corporal David Olsen of Phoenix, left, smiles as he receives a letter from his girlfriend from Corporal Edward O'Rourke of Mobile, Alabama, center, who was handing out mail to members of India Company, 3rd Battalion, 7th Marines, 1st Marines Division.

CITIZENSHIP

"**Our citizenship** in the United States is our national character. Our citizenship in any particular state is only our local distinction. By the latter we are known at home, by the former to the world. Our great title is AMERICANS . . . "

Thomas Paine

RIGHT

About 5,000 people participate in a rally in Omaha, Nebraska, despite the cold and wind, to show their support for America and its troops.

HOPE

"**Freedom** is the last, best hope of earth."

Abraham Lincoln

RIGHT

Union workers hold American flags in support of the U.S. military efforts in Iraq near the former World Trade Center site in New York.

"I wish you all well, may God bless you all. I am a veteran myself and I am not fighting in body, but my spirit and heart are with you all. Come home safely. Proud to be an American always and forever."

LETTER OF SUPPORT TO U.S. TROOPS

SACRIFICE

"**These are sacrifices** in a high calling—the defense of our nation and the peace of the world. Overcoming evil is the noblest cause and the hardest work. And the liberation of millions is the **fulfillment** of America's founding promise. The objectives we've set in this war are worthy of America, worthy of all the acts of heroism and generosity that have come before. Once again, we are applying the power of our country to ensure our security and to serve the cause of justice. And **we will prevail**."

GEORGE W. BUSH

LEFT

Miyuki Cawley, the wife of U.S. Marine Staff Sergeant James Cawley, holds the flag from her husband's casket in her lap during graveside services in Roy City, Utah.

to be free and that to be free means to be brave. Therefore do not take lightly the perils of war. Be convinced that to lightly the perils of war. Be convinced that to be happy means to be free and that to be free means to be brave. Therefore do not take lightly the perils of war. Therefore do not take lightly the perils of war. Be convinced that to be happy me

"**Be convinced** that to be happy means to be free and that to be free means to be brave. Therefore do not take lightly the **perils of war.**"

Thucydides

113

"The price of freedom is eternal vigilance."

Thomas Jefferson

"**Sending Americans into battle** is the most profound decision a President can make. The technologies of war have changed; the risks and suffering of war have not. For the brave Americans who bear the risk, no victory is free from sorrow. This nation fights reluctantly, because we know the cost and we dread the **days of mourning that always come.**"

GEORGE W. BUSH

Colonel Gene Fowler, left, installation chaplain at Fort Sill, is pictured next to the fallen comrade memorial display in Fort Sill, Oklahoma, following the memorial service for servicemen who were killed in the war in Iraq.

RED, WHITE AND BLUE

"If you are **ashamed to stand** by your colors, you had better **seek another flag.**"

Anonymous

New York Governor George Pataki speaks to thousands of union workers in Manhattan bearing American flags in support of U.S. military efforts in Iraq.

Iraqi forces captured Chief Warrant Officer David Williams, 30, and fellow Apache helicopter pilot Chief Warrant Officer Ronald Young Jr., 26, on March 24 after their aircraft was attacked by small-arms fire and landed behind Iraqi lines. The soldiers abandoned the helicopter, dove into a canal and swam away, but were caught by farmers waiting in a field with assault rifles. Iraqi TV later showed people celebrating near the downed helicopter.

After the two pilots were recovered safely, along with five other POWS, David Williams's wife, Michelle, who is also an Army pilot, said, "I feel like I'm watching a movie. I watch the news and the television, and I think it's going to hit me sometime soon."

LEFT

A large yellow ribbon is tied to an oak tree outside the home of the grandparents of ex-POW David Williams in Orlando, Florida.

Amid heavy security, former POW Jessica Lynch is carried from a C-17 transport plane at Andrews Air Force Base on April 12, 2003, in transit to Walter Reed Army Medical Center to receive medical treatment.

MIRACLES

"**Last night,** in one of the most **heroic operations** of this conflict, U.S. forces extracted Private First Class Jessica Lynch of West Virginia from captivity in an Iraqi hospital near Nasiriyah and returned her to American custody.

Today is **a day of great rejoicing** for Private Lynch, for her parents, Greg and Dee, for the rest of her family and friends, and for all West Virginians—and indeed for all Americans. Jessica Lynch's rescue is nothing short of a miracle. This operation is a tribute to the skill and heroism of our soldiers.

Jessica Lynch's story has **lifted our hearts,** and her rescue is a cause for rejoicing throughout the land."

EXCERPTS FROM SENATOR JAY ROCKEFELLER'S (D-WV), ADDRESS TO HIS SENATE

COLLEAGUES ABOUT THE MIRACULOUS RESCUE OF PFC. JESSICA LYNCH

Former POW Specialist Joseph Hudson adjusts an American flag during his arrival at Biggs Army Airfield at Fort Bliss in El Paso, Texas. Seven former prisoners of war returned home to a crowd of flag-waving family and friends, one week after they were rescued in Iraq.

Five members of the 507th Company took a wrong turn on March 23 near Nasiriyah and were captured by the Iraqis.

Two other U.S. soldiers were taken prisoner on March 24 after their Apache helicopter was shot down near Karbala in central Iraq.

Shortly after, the U.S. POWs were shown on Iraqi state television being interrogated by their captors. The pictures sent shockwaves throughout America, and Washington immediately accused the Iraqi authorities of breaching the Geneva Convention. Their families and the nation endured many days of uncertainty and agony over their fates.

On Sunday, April 13, the seven POWs were freed. POW Shoshana Johnson, 30, said Marines kicked in the door of a room where they were being held, shouting: "If you're an American, stand up!" All seven American soldiers stood up and were immediately swept away to safety by their rescuers.

The Rev. Ron Pracht summed up the nation's sentiment over the miraculous recovery: "For the good news . . . let there be great rejoicing!"

FREED POWs:

Specialist Edgar **Hernandez**, 21, of Mission, Texas

Specialist Joseph **Hudson**, 23, of Alamogordo, N.M.

Specialist Shoshana **Johnson**, 30, of El Paso

Private First Class Patrick **Miller**, 23, of Valley Center, Kansas

Chief Warrant Officer David **Williams**, 30, of Orlando

Chief Warrant Officer Ronald **Young** Jr., 26, of Lithia Springs, Georgia

Sergeant James Joseph **Riley**, 31, of Pennsauken, N.J.

HAPPY ENDINGS

"The happy ending is our national belief."

Mary McCarthy

"When Iraqi civilians looked into the faces of our service men and women, they saw strength and kindness and goodwill. When I look at the members of the United States military, I see the best of our country, and I am honored to be your commander in chief."

GEORGE W. BUSH